Pittsburgh Steelers Football

Progressive Trivia

Researched by Paul F. Wilson

Paul F. Wilson & Tom P. Rippey III, Editors

Kick The Ball, Ltd

Lewis Center, Ohio

*This book is dedicated to
Jody Ackerman; Jay Caldwell; Tracy Pavetti;
Damon, Lauren, AJ, Abbie & Alora Smith;
and my cousin Yolanda Fuller*

*And to our regular Steelers game watch crew:
Mike, Tyra & Greyson Flynn and Tyler Boyer;
Keith, Ashley, Hailey & Ian Barto;
and Kara Barto Eakin*

Go Steelers!

**Pittsburgh Steelers Football: Progressive Trivia;
First Edition 2011**

Published by
Kick The Ball, Ltd
8595 Columbus Pike, Suite 197
Lewis Center, OH 43035
www.ProgressiveTriviaBooks.com

Edited by: Paul F. Wilson & Tom P. Rippey
Designed and Formatted by Paul F. Wilson
Researched by: Paul F. Wilson

Copyright © 2011 by Kick The Ball, Ltd, Lewis Center, Ohio

ALL RIGHTS RESERVED. No part of this book may be reproduced or transmitted in any form whatsoever, electronic, or mechanical, including photocopying, recording, or by any informational storage or retrieval system without the expressed written, dated and signed permission from the copyright holder.

Trademarks and Copyrights: Kick The Ball, Ltd is not associated with any event, team, conference, or league mentioned in this book. All trademarks are the property of their respective owners. Kick The Ball, Ltd respects and honors the copyrights and trademarks of others. We use event, team, conference, or league names only as points of reference in our books. Names, statistics, and others facts obtained through public domain resources.

LIMIT OF LIABILITY/DISCLAIMER OF WARRANTY: THE RESEARCHER AND PUBLISHER HAVE USED GREAT CARE IN RESEARCHING AND WRITING THIS BOOK. HOWEVER, WE MAKE NO REPRESENTATION OR WARRANTIES AS TO THE COMPLETENESS OF ITS CONTENTS OR THEIR ACCURACY AND WE SPECIFICALLY DISCLAIM ANY IMPLIED WARRANTIES OF MERCHANTABILITY OR FITNESS FOR A PARTICULAR PURPOSE. WARRANTIES MAY NOT BE CREATED OR EXTENDED BY ANY SALES MATERIALS OR SALESPERSON OF THIS BOOK. NEITHER THE RESEARCHER NOR THE PUBLISHER SHALL BE LIABLE FOR ANY LOSS OF PROFIT OR ANY OTHER COMMERCIAL DAMAGES, INCLUDING BUT NOT LIMITED TO SPECIAL, INCIDENTAL, CONSEQUENTIAL, OR OTHER DAMAGES.

For information on ordering this book in bulk at reduced prices, please email us at pfwilson@progressivetriviabooks.com.

International Standard Book Number: 978-1-61320-030-8

Printed and Bound in the United States of America

10 9 8 7 6 5 4 3 2 1

Table of Contents

Questions and Answers 1-180……………..……….. Page 1

Questions and Answers 181-360…………………….. Page 31

Questions and Answers 361-540……..…………..…Page 61

Questions and Answers 541-720……..........………... Page 91

About
Progressive Trivia Books
by Kick The Ball, Ltd

Play *Pittsburgh Steelers Football: Progressive Trivia* by yourself or with others, either way we hope you enjoy playing.

Each page of this book presents six questions that relate in some way to one another. Likewise, each question progresses through that page's theme in a way that builds on the previous question's answer, or the previous question itself. In so doing, a more complete picture emerges about the subject matter of that set of six questions.

Questions can take the form of: multiple choice; true or false; yes or no; fill in the blank; or simply a question with no answer options at all. Each type of question challenges you in a unique way to test your knowledge of the team's history, great moments, traditions, key players and coaches, championships, individual and team records, and much more.

The answers to each set of questions are conveniently placed at the bottom of that page. You may want to *cover the answers prior to beginning a section* to avoid prematurily revealing an answer to yourself.

Although we have taken care to avoid errors in this book, from time to time they may occur. If you find one, we ask for your understanding and thank you for bringing it to our attention. Please email tprippey@progressivetriviabooks.com with any comments or observations. Thank you and we sincerely hope you enjoy playing *Pittsburgh Steelers Football: Progressive Trivia.*

All information in this book is valid as of the end of the 2010 season.

Pittsburgh Steelers Football

1) Who is the Steelers' all-time leading passer?

2) How many total passing yards did he have?

3) When did he break Pittsburgh's previous record?

4) Where did he set the record?

   A) Pittsburgh
   B) Buffalo
   C) Los Angeles
   D) Houston

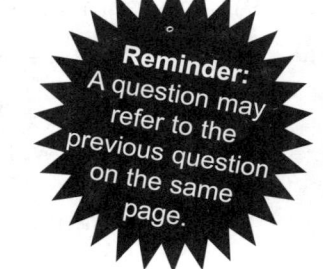

Reminder: A question may refer to the previous question on the same page.

5) What years did he play for the Steelers?

6) What ended his career?

Answers:

1) Terry Bradshaw
2) 27,989 yards
3) Nov. 24, 1975
4) D – Houston
5) 1970-83
6) He retired following an elbow injury.

Progressive Trivia

Pittsburgh Steelers Football

7) Who was the Steelers' most recent Super Bowl MVP?

8) How many times have Steelers players been named Super Bowl MVP?

9) The team's first Super Bowl MVP award was given to a Steeler in _____.

10) Where does Pittsburgh rank in its all-time number of Super Bowl MVPs compared to other NFL teams?

11) In which of their Super Bowl appearances did a Steelers player not win the MVP award?

12) Lynn Swann had 131 receiving yards in route to winning a Super Bowl MVP award against which team?

Answers:

7) Santonio Holmes
8) Six
9) 1975
10) Second; Dallas Cowboys rank No. 1
11) Super Bowl XXX and XLV
12) Dallas Cowboys

Progressive Trivia

Pittsburgh Steelers Football

13) When was the ground breaking for Heinz Field?

14) What was the stadium's cost of construction?

15) What is the stadium's seating capacity?

16) Who owns the stadium?

17) Who is the Steelers' co-tenant at the stadium?

18) The stadium's playing surface is artificial turf.

    A) True
    B) False

Answers:

13) June 18, 1999
14) $281 million
15) 65,500
16) Sports and Exhibition Authority of Pittsburgh and Allegheny County
17) University of Pittsburgh
18) B – False; It is natural grass.

Progressive Trivia

Pittsburgh Steelers Football

19) What was the original name of the Pittsburgh Steelers?

20) _____ founded the team.

21) Did the team play its first-ever game in 1933?

22) The team's name was officially changed to the Pittsburgh Steelers in what year?

23) What was the name of the team's first home field?

24) To which league did the team originally belong?

    A) AAFC
    B) AFL
    C) NFL
    D) PSFL

Answers:

19) Pittsburgh Pirates
20) Art Rooney
21) A – Yes
22) 1940
23) Forbes Field
24) C – NFL

Progressive Trivia

Pittsburgh Steelers Football

25) What year did the team logo, which is based on the Steelmark logo, make its debut on Steelers helmets?

26) The Steelers are the only NFL team whose logo appears on only one side of the team helmet.

    A) True
    B) False

27) On which side of the Steelers helmet does the logo appear?

28) Team helmets were what color when the logo was first added?

29) Why did the team change the color of their helmets to black?

30) What colors are the three four-pointed hypocycloids (astroids) that appear inside the logo?

Answers:

25) 1962
26) A – True
27) Right
28) Gold
29) To commemorate their first-ever postseason appearance and to highlight the new team logo
30) Gold, Red and Blue

Progressive Trivia

Pittsburgh Steelers Football

31) There are a total of 22 Pittsburgh Steelers players, coaches, contributors and administrators enshrined in the Pro Football Hall of Fame.

   A) True
   B) False

32) What year was the first Steeler enshrined into the Pro Football Hall of Fame?

33) How many Steelers were members of the Pro Football Hall of Fame's charter class?

34) Which of the following represented the Steelers in the charter class of the Pro Football Hall of Fame?

   A) Bert Bell
   B) Robert "Cal" Hubbard
   C) John "Blood" McNally
   D) All of the above

35) Art Rooney was a member of which class?

36) What rare distinction do Art and Dan Rooney hold in the Pro Football Hall of Fame?

Answers:

31) B – False; There are 24.
32) 1963
33) Three
34) D – All of the above
35) 1964
36) They are the second father-son combination in the Hall.

Progressive Trivia

Pittsburgh Steelers Football

37) How many draft picks did the Steelers have in the 2011 NFL Draft?

38) Who did Pittsburgh select with their only first-round selection of the 2011 draft?

39) The Steelers 2011 first round draft pick was a four-year player from which university?

   A) Michigan
   B) Ohio State
   C) Florida
   D) Texas

40) All time, how many players have the Steelers drafted out of Ohio State?

41) Who was the first-ever player the Steelers drafted from Ohio State?

42) What year did Pittsburgh draft its first-ever player from Ohio State?

Answers:

37) Seven
38) Cameron Heyward
39) B – Ohio State
40) 16
41) Jack Dugger
42) 1945

Progressive Trivia

Pittsburgh Steelers Football

43) The Steelers have made _____ all-time appearances in the Super Bowl?

44) Which other NFL team has made the same number of Super Bowl appearances as Pittsburgh?

45) What year did the Steelers play in their first-ever Super Bowl?

46) Did the Steelers travel to Miami, Fla. to play in Super Bowl IX?

    A) Yes
    B) No

47) What is the Steelers' winning percentage in Super Bowl games?

48) How many Super Bowl titles has the Steelers franchise won?

Answers:

43) Eight
44) Dallas Cowboys
45) 1975
46) B – No; New Orleans, La.
47) .750
48) Six

Progressive Trivia

Pittsburgh Steelers Football

49) Jason Gildon is the Steelers' all-time sacks leader.

   A) True
   B) False

50) How many sacks did he have?

51) How many seasons did he play in Pittsburgh?

52) Who is second on the all-time career sacks leaders list, Joe Greene or L.C. Greenwood?

53) How many career sacks does the No. 2 player on the list have?

54) Do any current Steelers rank in the top five of the team's all-time sacks leaders list?

   A) Yes
   B) No

Answers:

49) A – True
50) 77.0
51) 10 seasons from 1994-2003
52) L.C. Greenwood
53) 73.5
54) B – No

Progressive Trivia

Pittsburgh Steelers Football

55) How many jersey numbers has the Steelers organization officially retired?

56) Who wore the officially retired jersey number?

57) What jersey number did he wear while playing in Pittsburgh?

58) What position did he play for the Steelers?

59) What year was his jersey number officially retired?

60) How many jersey numbers are unofficially retired by the Steelers organization?

Answers:

55) One
56) Ernie Stautner
57) #70
58) Defensive Tackle
59) 1964
60) Eight

Progressive Trivia

Pittsburgh Steelers Football

61) Super Bowl XLIII between the Steelers and the Cardinals was played in the city of _____.

62) What was the name of the host stadium of the Super Bowl in 2009?

63) What was the final score of Super Bowl XLIII?

64) Who was the Super Bowl XLIII MVP?

65) Which Steeler declined President Obama's invitation to visit the White House following the Steelers victory in Super Bowl XLIII?

66) Did the Steelers defenseman identified above visit the White House when invited by George W. Bush in 2006?

Answers:

61) Tampa, Fla.
62) Raymond James Stadium
63) Steelers 27, Cardinals 23
64) Santonio Holmes
65) James Harrison
66) No

Progressive Trivia

Pittsburgh Steelers Football

67) Who owns the Steelers' individual record for the most career receiving touchdowns?

68) How many receiving touchdowns does he have?

　　A) 83
　　B) 89
　　C) 94
　　D) 98

69) His receptions were made over how many seasons?

70) When was his first season with the team?

71) From which school was he drafted?

72) In what country was he born?

Answers:

67) Hines Ward
68) A – 83
69) 13
70) 1998
71) Georgia
72) South Korea

Pittsburgh Steelers Football

73) When was the Steelers' record for the longest-ever field goal made set?

74) Who successfully kicked the field goal?

75) How many yards was the record-setting field goal?

76) Where was the record set?

    A) Oakland
    B) New Orleans
    C) Pittsburgh
    D) Kansas City

77) Was the record-setting field goal also the game-winning field goal that day?

    A) Yes
    B) No

78) Who was the holder for the record-setting field goal?

Answers:

73) Oct. 14, 2001
74) Kris Brown
75) 55
76) D – Kansas City
77) B – No
78) Josh Miller

Progressive Trivia

Pittsburgh Steelers Football

79) Who holds the Steelers' record for the highest single-season passing completion percentage (min. 250 attempts)?

80) When did he set the team record in the category?

81) What was his record completion percentage that season?

82) He completed _____ of _____ passes that year.

83) How many games did he play that season?

84) He is also second on the team's list for the highest passing completion percentage in a season.

   A) True
   B) False

Answers:

79) Ben Roethlisberger
80) 2009
81) 66.6 percent
82) 337, 506
83) 15
84) A – True; 66.4 percent in 2004

Progressive Trivia

Pittsburgh Steelers Football

85) The Steelers' team record for the most career touchdown passes is owned by which quarterback?

    A) Kordell Stewart
    B) Neil O'Donnell
    C) Ben Roethlisberger
    D) Terry Bradshaw

86) How many career touchdown passes did he complete?

87) How many seasons did it take to accumulate his record-setting career touchdown passes?

88) Which years did he spend with the Steelers?

89) His career total in the category is twice as high as the next highest Steelers QB on the list.

    A) True
    B) False

90) Does he also own the team records for the most touchdown passes in a season and in a game?

Answers:

85) D – Terry Bradshaw
86) 212
87) 14
88) 1970-83
89) B – False; Roethlisberger has 144.
90) No

Progressive Trivia

Pittsburgh Steelers Football

91) What is the Steelers' record for the most punt returns by a player in a single game?

92) Who set the record?

93) Against what team was the record set?

94) What year did he set the team record?

95) How many punt return yards did he gain that game?

    A) 79
    B) 83
    C) 97
    D) 105

96) Did his punt returns that day help him set the Steelers' single-season record in the category as well?

Answers:

91) 10
92) Theo Bell
93) Buffalo Bills
94) 1979
95) D – 105
96) No; He secured the No. 3 spot on the list, however.

Progressive Trivia

Pittsburgh Steelers Football

97) Franco Harris holds the Steelers' career record for the most 100-yard rushing games.

    A) True
    B) False

98) How many 100-yard rushing games does the career leader have?

99) When was his first season with the team?

100) When was his final season with the team?

101) How many 100-yard rushing games did Franco Harris have during his career in Pittsburgh?

102) Who is third on the Steelers' list for the category and how many 100-yard rushing games did he have?

Answers:

97) B – False; Jerome Bettis.
98) 50
99) 1996
100) 2005
101) 47
102) Willie Parker, 25

Progressive Trivia

Pittsburgh Steelers Football

103) Who was the Steelers' opponent in Super Bowl X?

104) Where was Super Bowl X played?

105) The Steelers defeated their Super Bowl X rival by 21 points.

   A) True
   B) False

106) Who was named Super Bowl X MVP?

107) Did the game's MVP set a then-Super Bowl record with 161 receiving yards?

108) Was Roger Staubach's final pass of the game intercepted in the end zone?

Answers:

103) Dallas Cowboys
104) Miami, Fla.
105) B – False; Final score was 21-17.
106) Lynn Swann
107) Yes; 4-161
108) Yes; By safety Mike Wagner

Progressive Trivia

Pittsburgh Steelers Football

109) How many yards is the longest interception return in Steelers history?

110) Who holds the Steelers' all-time record for the longest interception return?

111) When did he set the team record?

112) Against which team was the interception returned?

113) How many yards is the second longest interception return in Steelers history?

114) Who holds the record for the second longest interception return?

   A) Lawrence Timmons
   B) Glen Edwards
   C) Jack Hinkle
   D) Martin Kottler

Answers:

109) 99
110) Martin Kottler
111) Sept. 27, 1933
112) Chicago Cardinals
113) 91
114) C – Jack Hinkle

Progressive Trivia

Pittsburgh Steelers Football

115) The Steelers' single-game rushing yards record was set versus Cleveland.

   A) True
   B) False

116) Who set the record versus Cleveland that day?

117) When was the record in the category set?

118) How many carries did he have that game?

119) Did any of his rushing attempts result in a touchdown?

120) Did the Steelers win the ball game as a result of his record-setting performance?

Answers:

115) A – True
116) Willie Parker
117) Dec. 7, 2006
118) 32
119) Yes; One
120) Yes; Steelers 27, Browns 7

Progressive Trivia

Pittsburgh Steelers Football

121) John Stallworth shares the Steelers' record for the most 100-yard receiving games in a season with whom?

122) How many 100-yard receiving games in a season did they each have to set the team record?

123) What year did John Stallworth have his record-setting season?

124) Hines Ward has had four or more 100-yard receiving games in a season five times.

   A) True
   B) False

125) Yancey Thigpen had ___ 100-yard receiving games in 1997.

126) What honor did Yancey Thigpen earn as a result of his accomplishments in 1997?

Answers:

121) Mike Wallace
122) Seven
123) 1984
124) A – True; 5 (2009) and 4 (2002, 2005, 2008 and 2010)
125) Six
126) Pro Bowl Selection

Progressive Trivia

Pittsburgh Steelers Football

127) What are the most games the Steelers have ever won in a single season?

128) What year did the Steelers win the most games in franchise history?

129) Did the Steelers win 16 straight games from 2004-05?

130) Which team ended the Steelers' record consecutive wins streak?

131) Did the 2004 Steelers win 13 consecutive games?

132) Which team did the Steelers defeat to begin their win streak in 2004?

Answers:

127) 15
128) 2004
129) Yes
130) New England Patriots
131) No; They won 14 consecutive games.
132) Miami Dolphins

Progressive Trivia

Pittsburgh Steelers Football

133) _____ was the most recent Steeler to score four touchdowns in a single game.

134) What season did he set this mark?

135) Against which team did he score the four TDs?

136) Who is the only other Steeler to score four TDs in a single game?

137) What season did he accomplish the feat?

138) Against which team did he accomplish the feat?

Answers:

133) Roy Jefferson
134) 1968
135) Atlanta Falcons
136) Ray Mathews
137) 1954
138) Cleveland

Progressive Trivia

Pittsburgh Steelers Football

139) What is the Steelers' team record for the most fumbles lost in a single game?

140) To which opponent were the fumbles lost?

141) What season did this occur?

142) Did the Steelers win this game despite their team turnovers?

143) That year the Steelers went on to set a team record for the most fumbles lost in a season.

   A) True
   B) False

144) Which season was the team record for the most fumbles lost set?

Answers:

139) Seven
140) Cincinnati Bengals
141) 1979
142) No; Steelers 10, Bengals 34
143) False
144) 1950; 29 fumbles lost in 12 games

Progressive Trivia

Pittsburgh Steelers Football

145) What year was Art Rooney, Sr. born?

146) He was born in the state of _____?

147) Which college did he attend?

148) Which sport was Art Rooney not noted as having played?

   A) Hockey
   B) Football
   C) Baseball
   D) Boxing

149) What was Art Rooney, Sr.'s nickname?

150) Art Rooney, Sr. boxed in the 1920 Summer Olympics in Belgium.

   A) True
   B) False

Answers:

145) 1901; Jan. 27
146) Pennsylvania
147) Duquesne; He also attended Georgetown and IUP.
148) A – Hockey
149) The Chief
150) B – False; It was speculated that he could have.

Progressive Trivia

Pittsburgh Steelers Football

151) Which Steeler holds the team's record for the most career points scored?

152) How many career points did he score?

153) He played for the Steelers from 1982 through _____.

154) How many points after touchdown did he record?

155) How many field goals did he make?

156) He was selected to the Pro Bowl three times while playing for the Steelers.

   A) True
   B) False

Answers:

151) Gary Anderson
152) 1,343
153) 1994
154) 416
155) 309
156) A – True; 1983, 1985 and 1993

Progressive Trivia

Pittsburgh Steelers Football

157) The Steelers' career record for total yards from scrimmage is held by _____.

158) How many total yards did he have?

159) He was a Steeler from 1972 through which season?

    A) 1977
    B) 1979
    C) 1981
    D) 1983

160) Was his career total yards from scrimmage greater than John Stallworth's and Lynn Swan's combined?

161) Who is ranked second on the career leaders list for this category?

162) How many total yards from scrimmage does the No. 2 player on the list have?

Answers:

157) Franco Harris
158) 14,234
159) D – 1983
160) No; They combined for 14,368.
161) Hines Ward
162) 12,130

Progressive Trivia

Pittsburgh Steelers Football

163) Where did the Steelers set the team record for the most points scored in a game?

    A) Home
    B) Away

164) What team was visiting the Steelers that day?

165) What week was the game played?

166) Which team had the better record heading into the game?

167) How many points did the Steelers score in the fourth quarter?

168) What was the final score of the game?

Answers:

163) A – Home
164) New York Giants
165) Week 10
166) New York Giants; They were 6-3, Steelers were 3-6.
167) 28
168) Steelers 63, Giants 7

Progressive Trivia

Pittsburgh Steelers Football

169) Who holds the Steelers' record for the most passes had intercepted in a game?

   A) Terry Bradshaw
   B) Tommy Wade
   C) Mike Tomczak
   D) Kordell Stewart

170) Which team intercepted the passes?

171) How many passes did they intercept?

172) How many passing attempts did he have on the day?

173) How many passing touchdowns did he have?

174) Despite the interceptions, he still managed to pass for nearly 300 yards that game.

   A) True
   B) False

Answers:

169) B – Tommy Wade
170) Philadelphia Eagles
171) Seven
172) 38
173) One
174) A – True; 278 yards passing, 22 completions

Progressive Trivia

Pittsburgh Steelers Football

175) The Steelers' career record for the most consecutive points after touchdown made is over 200.

   A) True
   B) False

176) Who holds the team record in the category?

177) When did the streak begin?

178) When did the streak end?

179) Did the streak begin and end versus the same opponent?

180) Does he also hold the NFL record for the category?

Answers:

175) True; 202
176) Gary Anderson
177) Sept. 11, 1983
178) Dec. 4, 1988
179) No; Green Bay and Houston
180) No; 422 by Matt Stover

Progressive Trivia

Pittsburgh Steelers Football

181) All time, how many times have Steelers been selected to the Pro Bowl?

182) How many Steelers were selected to the Pro Bowl in 1951, the inaugural NFL Pro Bowl?

183) What is the highest number of Steelers to be selected to the Pro Bowl in a year?

184) What year were the most Steelers selected for the game?

185) Since 1951, how many times were no Steelers selected for the Pro Bowl in a year?

186) What season did no Steeler get selected for the Pro Bowl?

Answers:

181) 276
182) Three
183) 11
184) 1976
185) One
186) 2000

Progressive Trivia

Pittsburgh Steelers Football

187) What is the distance of the longest-ever punt in Steelers history?

    A) 71 yards
    B) 78 yards
    C) 80 yards
    D) 82 yards

188) The Steelers' longest punt was kicked by _____.

189) Pittsburgh was visiting which team the day he kicked the record-setting punt?

190) What year did he set the record?

191) Have Josh Miller and Bobby Joe Green both kicked 75-yard punts for the Steelers?

192) What year did Josh Miller kick his 75-yarder?

Answers:

187) D – 82 yards
188) Joe Geri
189) Green Bay Packers
190) 1949; Nov. 20
191) Yes
192) 1999; Dec. 2

Progressive Trivia

Pittsburgh Steelers Football

193) Did Jeff Reed kick more points after touchdown in his career as a Steeler than Gary Anderson?

194) Who kicked the third most points after touchdown in Steelers history?

195) How many PATs did he kick?

196) How many seasons was he in Pittsburgh?

197) How many total extra points did Gary Anderson kick in his NFL career?

198) Does Gary Anderson hold the NFL record for the most extra points made in a career?

Answers:

193) No; Reed had 307 to Anderson's 416.
194) Roy Gerela
195) 293
196) Eight
197) 820
198) No; George Blanda had 943 & Morten Andersen 849.

Progressive Trivia

Pittsburgh Steelers Football

199) What is Pittsburgh's team record for the most touchdowns in a single game?

200) Against which opponent did they accomplish this feat?

201) Where was this game played?

    A) Home
    B) Away

202) What is Pittsburgh's team record for the most touchdowns allowed in a game?

203) Which teams hold this record?

204) Where were these games played?

    A) Home
    B) Away

Answers:

199) Nine
200) New York Giants
201) A – Home; Nov. 30, 1952
202) Eight
203) San Diego and Green Bay
204) A – Home; SD Dec. 8, 1985, and GB Nov. 23, 1941

Progressive Trivia

Pittsburgh Steelers Football

205) Who was the Steelers' opponent in Super Bowl XL?

206) Which city hosted Super Bowl XL?

207) What is the name of the Stadium in which the game was played?

208) Did the Steelers ever trail in Super Bowl XL?

209) What was the name of the opposing quarterback?

210) What was the combined score of both teams?

Answers:

205) Seattle Seahawks
206) Detroit, Mich.
207) Ford Field
208) Yes; 0-3
209) Matt Hasselbeck
210) 31 points; Steelers 21, Seahawks 10

Progressive Trivia

Pittsburgh Steelers Football

211) _____ holds the Steelers' record for the most punt returns in a season.

212) What year did he set the team record for the category?

213) How many punt returns did he have that season?

214) Who holds the No. 2 spot on the list for the category?

215) How many punts did the No. 2 player return in a season to earn his place on the list?

216) What year was the No. 2 spot secured?

    A) 1990
    B) 1991
    C) 1995
    D) 1998

Answers:

211) Louis Lipps
212) 1984
213) 53
214) Andre Hastings
215) 48
216) C – 1995

Progressive Trivia

Pittsburgh Steelers Football

217) Who created The Terrible Towel?

218) What year did he create it?

219) Since 1996, what charity benefits from sales of The Terrible Towel and related products?

220) How much money has been raised for the charity from the sale of The Terrible Towel products since 1996?

221) What relationship did Myron Cope have with the Steelers?

   A) Broadcaster
   B) Team Physician
   C) Grounds Keeper
   D) Uniform Supplier

222) Who does Allegheny Valley School serve?

Answers:

217) Myron Cope
218) 1975
219) Allegheny Valley School
220) Over $3 million
221) A – Broadcaster
222) Persons with intellectual and developmental disabilities

Progressive Trivia

Pittsburgh Steelers Football

223) Who owns the Steelers' record for the most career interceptions?

224) How many career interceptions did he have?

225) He played for the Steelers from 1970 through _____.

226) Does Jack Butler have one fewer career interception than Mel Blount?

227) How many career interceptions does Jack Butler have?

228) How many seasons did it take him to accumulate his second-best number of interceptions?

Answers:

223) Mel Blount
224) 57
225) 1983
226) No
227) 52
228) Nine

Pittsburgh Steelers Football

229) Mike Wallace set the Steelers' record for the most yards receiving in a season.

   A) True
   B) False

230) What is the Steelers' record for the most yards receiving in a season?

231) When was the record set?

232) How many times does Yancey Thigpen appear in the top 10 spots of this category?

233) Who holds the No. 2 spot on the list?

234) He had _____ yards receiving in the _____ season.

Answers:

229) B – False; Yancey Thigpen
230) 1,398
231) 1997
232) Two; No. 1 and No. 5
233) John Stallworth
234) 1,395, 1984

Progressive Trivia

Pittsburgh Steelers Football

235) What is the Steelers' record for the most punts in a single game?

236) Who holds the record?

237) Against what team was the record set?

238) What year was the record set?

239) Mark Royals punted 11 times in two separate games in his career.

   A) True
   B) False

240) Who played more seasons with the Steelers, Josh Miller or Mark Royals?

Answers:

235) 12
236) Josh Miller
237) Cincinnati Bengals
238) 2000; Oct. 15
239) A – True
240) Josh Miller; Miller (1996-2003) and Royals (1992-94)

Progressive Trivia

Pittsburgh Steelers Football

241) Dick LeBeau is a graduate of which university?

242) Dick LeBeau is the innovator of the Steelers' "_____ blitz."

243) What season did LeBeau rejoin the Steelers?

244) What team did he coach immediately prior to returning to the Steelers?

245) What position did he play as an NFL player?

246) What year was he enshrined in the Pro Football Hall of Fame?

Answers:

241) Ohio State
242) zone
243) 2004
244) Buffalo Bills
245) Cornerback
246) 2010

Progressive Trivia

Pittsburgh Steelers Football

247) Has any Steeler ever returned a kick for greater than 100 yards?

248) Who holds the Steelers' record for the longest-ever kick return?

249) What year did he set the team record for the category?

250) What opposing team was on the wrong side of his record-setting kick return?

251) Who kicked the ball that he returned?

252) Did the record-setting kick return help the Steelers secure a victory that day?

Answers:

247) Yes; 101 yards
248) Don McCall
249) 1969; Nov. 23
250) Minnesota Vikings
251) Gene Mingo
252) No; Steelers 14, Vikings 52

Progressive Trivia

Pittsburgh Steelers Football

253) What are the most penalties by the Steelers in a single game?

254) Did the penalties occur in a home or an away game?

255) The penalties resulted in a loss of _____ yards.

256) How many penalties did the Steelers opposition incur that game?

257) The 1977 Steelers also hold the record for the most penalties in a season.

   A) True
   B) False

258) How many penalties did they amass that season?

Answers:

253) 17
254) Away; at Baltimore on Oct. 30, 1977
255) 122
256) Three
257) A – True
258) 122

Progressive Trivia

Pittsburgh Steelers Football

259) Does a running back or quarterback hold the Steelers' career record for the highest rushing average?

260) Who holds the record?

261) What was his career rushing average?

262) Who is second on the career list in the category?

263) What was his career rushing average?

264) Who is the highest ranked back on the list?

Answers:

259) Quarterback
260) Kordell Stewart
261) 5.23 yards per carry
262) Terry Bradshaw
263) 5.05 yards per carry
264) Bill Dudley; Half back, 4.39 yards per carry

Progressive Trivia

Pittsburgh Steelers Football

265) How many Steelers quarterbacks have thrown five touchdown passes in a single game?

266) Which of the following Steelers QBs did not throw five TDs in a game?

   A) Ben Roethlisberger
   B) Bubby Brister
   C) Terry Bradshaw
   D) Mark Malone

267) Against which AFC North division rival did Ben Roethlisberger complete five TD passes?

268) What year did Ben Roethlisberger accomplish this feat?

269) Did Big Ben throw any interceptions that day?

270) Were the Steelers victorious that day?

Answers:

265) Three
266) B – Bubby Brister
267) Baltimore Ravens
268) 2007
269) No
270) Yes; Steelers 38, Ravens 7

Progressive Trivia

Pittsburgh Steelers Football

271) James Harrison owns the Steelers' record for the most quarterback sacks in a single season.

   A) True
   B) False

272) How many QB sacks make up the team record?

273) What season was the record set?

274) How many games did he play in that season?

275) _____ had the second most sacks that season.

276) How many sacks did the No. 2 player have?

Answers:

271) A – True
272) 16
273) 2008
274) 15
275) LaMarr Woodley
276) 11.5

Progressive Trivia

Pittsburgh Steelers Football

277) How many career 100-yard receiving games has Hines Ward had?

278) Does Hines Ward or John Stallworth hold the Steelers' record in the category?

279) How many career games with 100 yards receiving did John Stallworth have?

280) Which of the above players has spent the most seasons with the team?

281) Does Hines Ward have more 100-yard receiving games than Plaxico Burress, Lynn Swann and Yancey Thigpen combined?

282) Does John Stallworth have more 100-yard receiving games than Louis Lipps and Plaxico Burress combined?

Answers:

277) 29
278) Hines Ward
279) 25
280) John Stallworth; Stallworth 14 seasons, Ward 13
281) No; They have 31 games combined.
282) No; They have 27 games combined.

Progressive Trivia

Pittsburgh Steelers Football

283) A Steelers kicker has made six field goals in a single game.

   A) True
   B) False

284) Who has accomplished this feat?

285) Against with team did Jeff Reed do it?

286) Did the Steelers win that contest?

287) Against which team did Gary Anderson do it?

288) Did the Steelers win that game?

Answers:

283) A – True
284) Jeff Reed and Gary Anderson
285) Jacksonville Jaguars
286) Yes; Steelers 25, Jaguars 23
287) Denver Broncos
288) Yes; Steelers 39, Broncos 21

Progressive Trivia

Pittsburgh Steelers Football

289) Who holds the Steelers' record for the most consecutive games intercepting a pass?

290) How many consecutive games did he intercept a pass during the streak?

291) What season did he set that mark?

292) Against what team did the streak begin?

293) Did he have two or more INTs in any of those games?

294) Against which team did the streak end?

Answers:

289) Mel Blount
290) Six
291) 1975
292) Cincinnati Bengals; Week 7
293) Yes; 2 versus Kansas City Chiefs and New York Jets
294) Cincinnati Bengals; He had no INTs in Week 13

Progressive Trivia

Pittsburgh Steelers Football

295) Who was Pittsburgh's first-ever draft selection?

296) From which university was he taken?

297) Which round of the 1936 draft was he taken?

298) Was he taken amongst the top three picks of that year's draft?

299) How many seasons did he play for the Steelers?

300) Was he the first-ever player from Notre Dame to be drafted in the first round of a draft?

Answers:

295) Bill Shakespeare
296) Notre Dame
297) First
298) Yes; Pick No. 3
299) Zero; He opted to begin a business career instead.
300) Yes

Progressive Trivia

Pittsburgh Steelers Football

301) What was the origin of the Steelers' defensive front four's nickname of the "Steel Curtain"?

302) What year was the nickname popularized?

303) "Mean" Joe Greene, L.C. Greenwood, Ernie Holmes and Dwight White were the original 1970s Steel Curtain.

   A) True
   B) False

304) Were L.C. Greenwood and Joe Greene named to the NFL's 1970s All-Decade Team?

305) How many members of the original Steel Curtain are in the Pro Football Hall of Fame?

306) Which member is enshrined in Canton?

Answers:

301) Radio station fan contest
302) 1971
303) A – True
304) Yes
305) One
306) #75 "Mean" Joe Greene

Progressive Trivia

Pittsburgh Steelers Football

307) Who holds the Steelers' record for the most career receptions?

308) How many career receptions does he have?

309) He accumulated his team-leading receptions from _____.

310) How many times has he been named Steelers MVP?

311) How many times has he been named a Second Team All-Pro?

312) He is a five-time Pro Bowl selection.

    A) True
    B) False

Answers:

307) Hines Ward
308) 954
309) 1998-2010
310) Three; 2002-03 and 2005
311) Three; 2002-04
312) B – False; Four-time selection, 2001-04

Progressive Trivia

Pittsburgh Steelers Football

313) Mike Tomlin is the _____ all-time head coach of the Pittsburgh Steelers.

314) What year did Tomlin take the helm as head coach?

315) How old was he when he was hired as the coach of the Steelers?

316) Mike Tomlin is the youngest-ever coach to win a Super Bowl title.

   A) True
   B) False

317) Including Mike Tomlin, how many NFL head coaches have won the Super Bowl within two seasons of becoming an NFL head coach?

318) What was the Steelers' regular-season record in Tomlin's second year as head coach?

Answers:

313) 16th
314) 2007
315) 34
316) A – True
317) Seven
318) 12-4

Progressive Trivia

Pittsburgh Steelers Football

319) What year was the Steelers' record for the longest punt return set?

320) Against which team was the record set?

321) What Steelers return man set the record?

322) How many yards was his record-setting punt return?

323) Did he score a touchdown on the punt return?

324) He had two punt returns on the day. How many yards was his other return?

Answers:

319) 1964
320) New York Giants
321) Brady Keys
322) 90
323) No
324) Three

Progressive Trivia

Pittsburgh Steelers Football

325) The Steelers played the _____ in Super Bowl XIII.

326) Where was the Super Bowl held that season?

327) Did more than 80,000 fans attend the game?

328) Did a player from either team rush for greater than 100 yards that day?

329) Who scored the Steelers' first points of the game?

330) Pittsburgh defeated Dallas by how many points?

Answers:

325) Dallas Cowboys
326) Miami, Fla.; Miami Orange Bowl
327) No; 78,656 official attendance
328) No; Tony Dorsett was closest with 96 yards.
329) John Stallworth; 28-yard pass from Terry Bradshaw
330) Four

Progressive Trivia

Pittsburgh Steelers Football

331) Who holds the Steelers' record for the most points after touchdown made in a game?

   A) Matt Bahr
   B) Norm Johnson
   C) Gary Kerkorian
   D) Gary Anderson

332) How many extra points did he make to set the team record?

333) What year was the record set?

334) Against which team was the record set?

335) What is the name of the other Steelers player who kicked an extra point that day?

336) What was his normal position during extra point attempts?

Answers:

331) C – Gary Kerkorian
332) Eight
333) 1952; Nov. 30
334) New York Giants
335) Ray Matthews
336) Holder, They decided on the field to switch roles.

Progressive Trivia

Pittsburgh Steelers Football

337) How many Steelers were named to the NFL's 1970s All-Decade Team?

338) Six Steelers were named to the First Team.

   A) True
   B) False

339) How many players were named to the Second Team?

340) Was Coach Chuck Noll named to the All-Decade Team?

341) Which organization selected the 1970s All-Decade Team?

342) Lynn Swann received the third most votes (21) of all the players selected for the team. Who received the most?

Answers:

337) Nine
338) B – False; Three, Swann, Greene and Ham
339) Five; Bradshaw, Harris, Webster, Greenwood and Lambert
340) Yes, Second Team Coach
341) Pro Football Hall of Fame
342) Ray Guy; 24 votes

Progressive Trivia

Pittsburgh Steelers Football

343) How many times have the Steelers passed for five touchdowns in a single game?

344) The Steelers completed five touchdown passes against Baltimore on two occasions.

   A) True
   B) False

345) Against which team was the most recent occurrence?

346) When was the first-ever occurrence?

347) How many of these games included more than one Steeler with a TD pass?

348) Excluding Ben Roethlisberger, who was the most recent Steelers QB to accomplish this feat?

Answers:

343) Seven
344) B – False; Twice at Atlanta
345) Baltimore Ravens; Nov. 5, 2007
346) 1952; Nov. 30
347) Four
348) Mark Malone; 1985 vs. Indianapolis Colts

Progressive Trivia

Pittsburgh Steelers Football

349) The Steelers' record for the most rushing yards in a career is _____.

350) Who owns the team record in the category?

351) How many seasons did he don the Steelers' black and gold?

352) Who holds the No. 2 spot in the category?

353) How many rushing yards did he gain?

354) Did he play more or fewer seasons in Pittsburg than the No. 1 rusher?

Answers:

349) 11,950
350) Franco Harris
351) 12
352) Jerome Bettis
353) 10,571
354) Fewer; 10 seasons

Progressive Trivia

Pittsburgh Steelers Football

355) What is considered a perfect passer rating in the NFL?

356) How many times has a Steelers QB obtained a perfect passer rating in a game?

357) Who was the first-ever Steelers QB to have a perfect passer rating in a game?

358) Who was the most recent Steelers QB to do it?

359) What is the Steelers' record for the highest passer rating for a season?

360) Who owns that record?

Answers:

355) 158.3
356) Four
357) Terry Bradshaw; Dec. 19, 1976, vs. Baltimore Colts
358) Ben Roethlisberger; Dec. 20, 2007, vs. St. Louis Rams
359) 104.1
360) Ben Roethlisberger; 2007

Progressive Trivia

Pittsburgh Steelers Football

361) The Steelers' individual record for the most rushing attempts in a game was set versus Cincinnati.

    A) True
    B) False

362) When was the record set?

363) Who set the record?

364) How many rushing attempts did he have?

365) How many yards did he gain that day?

366) What was his longest run for the day?

Answers:

361) A – True
362) 1976; Oct. 17
363) Franco Harris
364) 41
365) 143
366) 13 yards

Progressive Trivia

Pittsburgh Steelers Football

367) Have the Steelers team helmets ever been green and white?

368) In which season where the team helmets green and white?

369) Why did the team wear green and white that season?

370) What was the unofficial name of the combined team that season?

371) By what name do official NFL record books refer to the 1943 combined team?

372) Why did the combined team wear the Eagles' uniforms?

Answers:

367) Yes
368) 1943
369) Due to the temporary merger with the Philadelphia Eagles
370) Steagles
371) Phil-Pitt Combine
372) As a cost-saving measure

Progressive Trivia

Pittsburgh Steelers Football

373) Was Super Bowl IX played in Tiger Stadium?

374) What was the host city for the game?

375) Who was the Steelers' opponent in Super Bowl IX?

376) How did the Steelers score there first points of the game?

   A) Safety
   B) Field Goal
   C) Touchdown Pass
   D) Touchdown Run

377) Who was named MVP of Super Bowl IX?

378) Franco Harris rushed for _____ yards and one touchdown in Super Bowl IX.

Answers:

373) No; Tulane Stadium
374) New Orleans
375) Minnesota Vikings
376) A – Safety
377) Franco Harris
378) 158

Progressive Trivia

Pittsburgh Steelers Football

379) Antwaan Randle El returned five punts for touchdowns during his career in Pittsburgh.

   A) True
   B) False

380) Were his punt returns for touchdowns good enough to set the Steelers' record for the category?

381) Who holds the No. 2 spot on the Steelers' career list in the category?

382) How many put returns for TDs do they have?

383) Steelers players returned ___ punts for touchdowns in 2010.

384) Who was the most recent Steeler to return a punt for a touchdown?

Answers:

379) B – False; Four
380) Yes
381) Louis Lipps and Ray Matthews
382) Three
383) Zero
384) Santonio Holmes; 2006

Progressive Trivia

Pittsburgh Steelers Football

385) What year was the Steelers' record for the highest kickoff return average set?

386) Who set the record?

387) What was his kickoff return average that season?

388) Mel Blount holds the No. 2 spot on the list.

    A) True
    B) False

389) What is the second highest average on the list?

390) Stefan Logan is the most recent player to be added to the top 10 list for the category. He is ranked sixth with a _____ average in _____.

Answers:

385) 1952
386) Lynn Chandnois
387) 35.2
388) B – False; Gary Ballman
389) 31.7
390) 26.7, 2009

Progressive Trivia

Pittsburgh Steelers Football

391) What are the most yards passing by a Steelers QB at Heinz Field?

392) Who holds the Heinz Field record for that category?

393) What are the most yards receiving by a Steeler at Heinz Field?

394) Who holds the Heinz Field record for that category?

395) What is the record for the most yards rushing at Heinz Field?

396) Who holds the Heinz Field record for that category?

Answers:

391) 503
392) Ben Roethlisberger
393) 253
394) Plaxico Burress
395) 223
396) Willie Parker

Progressive Trivia

Pittsburgh Steelers Football

397) Who holds the Steelers' record for the most field goal attempts in a season?

   A) Gary Anderson
   B) Kris Brown
   C) Roy Gerela
   D) None of the above

398) What year did he set the team record for the category?

399) How many field goat attempts did he have?

400) Who is second on the Steelers' single-season list for the category?

401) How many field goal attempts did the No. 2 player have?

402) What year did he secure the No. 2 spot on the list?

Answers:

397) B – Kris Brown
398) 2001
399) 44
400) Roy Gerela
401) 43
402) 1973

Progressive Trivia

Pittsburgh Steelers Football

403) "Here We Go" is an unofficial fight song of the Pittsburgh Steelers.

    A) True
    B) False

404) Who wrote the song?

405) What year was it written?

406) How long did the song's writer say it took to write the song?

407) Is Coach Tomlin referenced in recent versions of the song?

408) How many copies of the song have been sold since its release?

Answers:

403) A – True
404) Roger Wood
405) 1994
406) 20 minutes
407) Yes
408) 120,000

Progressive Trivia

Pittsburgh Steelers Football

409) Who was the first black player to play for the Steelers?

410) What year did he play for the team?

411) He was just one of two black players in the entire NFL that season.

   A) True
   B) False

412) How many games did he play for the then-Pittsburgh Pirates?

413) What college did he attend prior to joining the team?

414) The year after he was cut from the team's roster, did he became the head football coach at Bluefield State College?

Answers:

409) Ray Kemp
410) 1933
411) A – True
412) Three
413) Duquesne
414) Yes

Progressive Trivia

Pittsburgh Steelers Football

415) What is the Steelers' team record for the most yards gained rushing?

416) The record was set against the _____.

417) When was the record set?

418) How many rushes did the team have that game?

419) Did Franco Harris or Sidney Thornton have the most rushing attempts in the game?

420) Who won the game?

Answers:

415) 361
416) Cleveland Browns
417) Oct. 7, 1979
418) 45
419) Franco Harris had 19 to Sidney Thornton's 18.
420) Pittsburgh; Steelers 51, Browns 35

☆ Progressive Trivia ☆

Pittsburgh Steelers Football

421) Is the Steelers' record for the most passing attempts in a game over or under 60?

422) Which Steelers QB had the most passing attempts in a single game?

423) Against which team was the record set?

   A) Houston Texans
   B) San Diego Chargers
   C) Miami Dolphins
   D) Cleveland Browns

424) How many pass completions did he have that day?

425) How many TD passes did he complete that day?

426) _____ won the game.

Answers:

421) Under; 57
422) Tommy Maddox
423) A – Houston Texans
424) 30
425) Zero
426) Houston; Steelers 6, Texans 24

Progressive Trivia

Pittsburgh Steelers Football

427) Neil O'Donnell holds the Steelers' record for the highest career passer rating.

　　A) True
　　B) False

428) What is the Steelers' record for the highest career passer rating?

429) How many seasons are represented in this rating?

430) Who is ranked second in the category?

431) What is his career passer rating?

432) How many seasons are represented in his rating?

Answers:

427) B – False; Ben Roethlisberger
428) 92.5
429) Six; 2004-10
430) Neil O'Donnell
431) 81.6
432) Six

Progressive Trivia

Pittsburgh Steelers Football

433) Who set the Steelers' record for the most consecutive field goals made?

434) How many consecutive field goals did he make?

435) Were his consecutive field goals made in a single season or over two seasons?

436) When were they kicked?

437) What is the record for the second most consecutive field goals made in Steelers history?

438) _____ holds the No. 2 spot on the list for this category.

Answers:

433) Jeff Reed
434) 22
435) Over two seasons
436) 2004-05
437) 19
438) Gary Anderson

Progressive Trivia

Pittsburgh Steelers Football

439) Has Ben Roethlisberger ever passed for over 4,000 yards in a season?

440) Is Big Ben ranked No. 1 on the Steelers' list for the most yards passing in a season?

441) What year was the team's record set?

442) What is the next highest number of yards passing he had in a season?

443) Was that good enough to capture the No. 2 spot on the Steelers' list for this category?

444) How many times does Ben Roethlisberger appear on the Steelers' top 10 list for this category?

Answers:

439) Yes; 4,328
440) Yes
441) 2009
442) 3,513
443) No; Terry Bradshaw, 3,724 yards passing in 1979
444) Five; Nos. 1, 3, 6, 8 and 9

Progressive Trivia

Pittsburgh Steelers Football

445) All time, how many tie games have the Steelers had?

446) Have any of them ended in a 0-0 tie?

447) What was the highest score of any of the Steelers' tie games?

448) When was the most recent tie game they played in?

449) Against which team was the game played?

450) Since 1974 there have been 17 tie games played in the NFL; the Steelers have played in two of them.

   A) True
   B) False

Answers:

445) 21
446) Yes; Oct. 22, 1933, at Cincinnati
447) 35-35; Sept. 22, 1974, at Denver
448) 2002; Nov. 10
449) Atlanta Falcons
450) A – True

Progressive Trivia

Pittsburgh Steelers Football

451) _____ holds the Steelers' career and season records for the most TDs on kickoff returns.

452) How many TDs on kickoff returns did he score in his career in Pittsburgh?

453) What seasons did he play for the Steelers?

454) Which season did he score two TDs on kickoff returns?

455) Have any other Steelers scored two TDs on kickoff returns in their careers?

456) Who was the most recent Steeler to run a kickoff return for a TD?

Answers:

451) Lynn Chandnois
452) Three
453) 1950-66
454) 1952
455) Yes; Larry Anderson and Will Blackwell
456) Antonio Brown; Sept. 19, 2010, at Tennessee

Progressive Trivia

Pittsburgh Steelers Football

457) Bill Dudley holds the Steelers' record for the most interception return yards in a season.

   A) True
   B) False

458) What year did he set the mark?

459) How many interception return yards did he have that season?

460) Did Chad Scott amass over or under 225 interception return yards in 2001?

461) What position does he hold on the leaders list for this category?

462) Glen Edwards accumulated _____ interception return yards in 1973.

Answers:

457) A – True
458) 1946
459) 242
460) Under; 204
461) No. 2
462) 183; Ranked No. 3 in the category

Progressive Trivia

Pittsburgh Steelers Football

463) The Steelers' team record for the most first downs in a game is _____.

464) What year was the team record set?

465) Which opponent gave up those first downs?

466) What is the team record for the most first downs in a season?

467) What season did they set that mark?

468) Who was the starting QB for the Steelers that season?

Answers:

463) 36
464) 1979; Nov. 25
465) Cleveland Browns
466) 344
467) 1995
468) Neil O'Donnell

Progressive Trivia

Pittsburgh Steelers Football

469) Franco Harris scored exactly 100 touchdowns in his career in Pittsburgh.

   A) True
   B) False

470) What is his rank on the Steelers' career leaders list?

471) How many touchdowns has Hines Ward scored?

472) He is ranked _____ of all time.

473) Who holds the No. 3 spot on the list?

474) With how many touchdowns is he credited?

Answers:

469) A – True
470) No. 1
471) 84
472) Second
473) Jerome Bettis
474) 80

Pittsburgh Steelers Football

475) What is the Steelers' all-time record on Monday Night Football?

476) What year was their first-ever MNF game?

477) Where was that game played?

478) The Steelers defeated the Cincinnati Bengals 21-10 to win that game.

   A) True
   B) False

479) When was the most recent season the Steelers played two MNF games?

480) When was the most recent season they did not play on Monday night?

Answers:

475) 39-22
476) 1970; Nov. 2
477) Pittsburgh
478) A – True
479) 2007; Week 9 and Week 12
480) 2004

Progressive Trivia

Pittsburgh Steelers Football

481) Which Steeler has maintained the highest field goal percentage for a season?

    A) Jeff Reed
    B) Norm Johnson
    C) Gary Anderson
    D) Kris Brown

482) He set the Steelers' record in the category in _____.

483) What average did he carry that season?

484) Does Jeff Reed occupy three of the top five spots in the category?

485) What is the second highest field goal percentage in team history?

486) What is the third highest?

Answers:

481) C – Gary Anderson
482) 1993
483) 93.3
484) Yes; Nos. 2, 3 and 5
485) 92.0
486) 89.5

Progressive Trivia

Pittsburgh Steelers Football

487) What year was Super Bowl XXX played?

488) Where was the game played?

489) Who was the Steelers' opponent in the game?

490) The opposition scored three times before the Steelers got on the board.

   A) True
   B) False

491) Despite leading most statistical categories, did the Steelers still lose the game?

492) What was the final score of the game?

Answers:

487) 1996
488) Tempe, Ariz.
489) Dallas Cowboys
490) A – True
491) Yes
492) Steelers 17, Cowboys 27

Progressive Trivia

Pittsburgh Steelers Football

493) The Steelers have played in _____ overtime games in franchise history.

494) What is their all-time record in OT games?

495) The Steelers have a winning record on the road in OT games.

   A) True
   B) False

496) How many of the Steelers' postseason games have gone into overtime?

497) Did the Steelers win their most recent postseason overtime game?

498) What team did they defeat in that game?

Answers:

493) 40
494) 22-16-2
495) B – False; 11-14-1
496) Four
497) Yes
498) New York Jets; Steelers 20, Jets 17

Progressive Trivia

Pittsburgh Steelers Football

499) What year was the Steelers' record for the most passes had intercepted set?

500) Which Steelers QB set the record that year?

501) How many interceptions did he throw?

502) Is Ben Roethlisberger ranked No. 2 in the category?

503) How many interceptions did the No. 2 ranked player throw?

504) What year did that occur?

Answers:

499) 1955
500) Jim Finks
501) 26
502) No; Terry Bradshaw
503) 25
504) 1979

Progressive Trivia

Pittsburgh Steelers Football

505) Is the Steelers' team record for the fewest net yards gained under or over 50?

506) Against which team did the record low take place?

507) The year was _____.

508) How many times was Bubby Brister sacked in the game?

509) How many yards did the Steelers lose on those sacks?

510) Were the Steelers held scoreless in the game?

Answers:

505) Over; 53
506) Cleveland Browns
507) 1989; Sept. 10
508) Six
509) 67
510) Yes; Steelers 0, Browns 51

Progressive Trivia

Pittsburgh Steelers Football

511) How many times have Steelers receivers had 200 or more yards receiving in a single game?

512) Who was the most recent Steeler to exceed 200?

513) Hines Ward appears _____ times on the Steelers top 10 list for the most yards receiving in a game.

514) Do any current Steelers receivers appear on the list?

515) Excluding Plaxico Burress, who is the most recent Steeler to appear on the list?

516) What year did he earn his spot on the list?

Answers:

511) Four
512) Plaxico Burress; 253 in 2002
513) Zero
514) No
515) Yancey Thigpen
516) 1997; 196 yards receiving vs. Jacksonville Jaguars

Progressive Trivia

Pittsburgh Steelers Football

517) Who was the Steelers' MVP in 2010?

518) Who was the first-ever team MVP?

519) How many times have the Steelers named Co-MVPs?

520) Has a kicker or punter ever been named the team MVP?

521) How many times did Lynn Swan receive the honor?

522) Have more defensive linemen or offensive linemen received the honor?

Answers:

517) Troy Polamalu
518) Roy Jefferson; 1969
519) Three; 1988, 2002 and 2005
520) Yes; Gary Anderson, 1983
521) Zero
522) Defensive linemen; two to zero

Progressive Trivia

Pittsburgh Steelers Football

523) Which Steeler holds the team record for the most 100-yard rushing games in a season?

   A) Jerome Bettis
   B) Willie Parker
   C) Franco Harris
   D) Barry Foster

524) How many 100-yard rushing games did he have in a season?

525) What year did he accomplish this feat?

526) Who holds the No. 2 and No. 3 spots on the list?

527) How many 100-yard rushing games did he have to secure those spots?

528) _____ also appears two times in the top five players on the list.

Answers:

523) D – Barry Foster
524) 12
525) 1992
526) Jerome Bettis
527) 10; 1997 and 1996
528) Willie Parker; Nos. 4 and 5

Progressive Trivia

Pittsburgh Steelers Football

529) What is the coldest recorded temperature for a Steelers game?

530) Where was the game played?

  A) Green Bay
  B) Cincinnati
  C) Chicago
  D) Pittsburgh

531) Did the Steelers prevail that day?

532) What was the temperature for the second coldest game on record?

533) Was this game played in Pittsburgh?

534) What was the final score?

Answers:

529) 2 degrees
530) B – Cincinnati
531) No; 10-17 loss
532) 5 degrees
533) Yes
534) Steelers 28, Patriots 10

Progressive Trivia

Pittsburgh Steelers Football

535) Who holds the Steelers' career record for the most punts?

536) How many career punts did he have in Pittsburgh?

537) How many seasons was he a Steeler?

538) How many career punts did the player in the No. 2 spot have?

539) Who is ranked second on the career list?

540) He played for the Steelers from 1968 to _____.

Answers:

535) Josh Miller
536) 574
537) Eight
538) 572
539) Bobby Walden
540) 1977

Progressive Trivia

Pittsburgh Steelers Football

541) Who was the first Steeler awarded The Chief Award?

542) What year did he receive the award?

543) The award is named for whom?

544) What does the award recognize?

      A) Team Captain
      B) Off-the-field Leadership
      C) Locker Room Leadership
      D) Most Helpful to the Media

545) How often is the award given?

546) Have two Steelers ever received the award in the same year?

Answers:

541) Dan Rooney
542) 1988
543) Art Rooney
544) D – Most Helpful to the Media
545) Annually
546) Yes, Jerome Bettis and Deshea Townsend, 2000

Progressive Trivia

Pittsburgh Steelers Football

547) Which stadium hosted Super Bowl XLV?

548) Official attendance was over or under 100,000?

549) Which NFC division did the Steelers' opponent represent?

550) The Steelers were playing for their _____ Super Bowl victory, while Green Bay was playing for their _____.

551) What was the final margin of victory?

552) Who was awarded Super Bowl MVP?

Answers:

547) Cowboys Stadium
548) Over; 103,219
549) NFC North
550) Seventh, Fourth
551) Six Points
552) Aaron Rodgers

Progressive Trivia

Pittsburgh Steelers Football

553) Rod Woodson holds the Steelers' record for the most interceptions in a game.

   A) True
   B) False

554) How many interceptions were made by a player in a game to set the record?

555) Who holds the record?

556) Who was the Steelers' opponent the day he set the record?

557) What year was the record set?

558) Did he return any of his interceptions for a TD?

Answers:

553) B – False
554) Four
555) Jack Butler
556) Washington Redskins
557) 1953; Dec. 13
558) Yes; One, to give the Steelers a 14-13 victory

Progressive Trivia

Pittsburgh Steelers Football

559) What is the Steelers' career record for the highest punt return average?

560) Who holds the record?

561) When did he set the record?

562) Who is ranked No. 2?

563) What was his career punt return average?

564) How many seasons did he spend in Pittsburgh?

Answers:

559) 14.9
560) Bobby Gage
561) 1949-50
562) Bill Dudley
563) 14.4
564) Five

Progressive Trivia

Pittsburgh Steelers Football

565) What year was Three Rivers Stadium opened?

566) Did the Steelers win their first-ever regular-season game in Three Rivers Stadium?

567) Who did they play that game?

568) What was the final score?

569) The Steelers played their final game at Three Rivers Stadium in _____.

570) Did the Steelers win their final game at Three Rivers?

Answers:

565) 1970
566) No
567) Houston Oilers
568) Steelers 7, Oilers 19
569) 2000; Dec. 16
570) Yes; Steelers 24, Redskins 3

Progressive Trivia

Pittsburgh Steelers Football

571) What is the Steelers' team record for the most sacks in a game?

572) How many times have the Steelers recorded 10 team sacks in a game?

573) What was the most recent team to give up 10 sacks in a game to the Steelers?

574) The year was _____.

575) What is the Steelers' team record for the most sacks allowed in a game.

576) Which of the following teams recorded the record number of team sacks against the Steelers on Nov. 20, 1966?

  A) Dallas Cowboys
  B) St. Louis Cardinals
  C) New York Giants
  D) Washington Redskins

Answers:

571) 10
572) Four
573) Tampa Bay Buccaneers
574) 2001; Oct. 21
575) 12
576) A – Dallas Cowboys

Progressive Trivia

Pittsburgh Steelers Football

577) Who holds the Steelers' record for the most yards rushing in a season?

    A) Jerome Bettis
    B) Willie Parker
    C) Barry Foster
    D) Franco Harris

578) He set the record in _____.

579) How many yards rushing did he have that year?

580) Did he play all 16 games for the Steelers that season?

581) How many rushing attempts did he have?

582) Did his performance earn him a trip to the Pro Bowl?

Answers:

577) C – Barry Foster
578) 1992
579) 1,690
580) Yes; With 15 starts
581) 390
582) Yes

Progressive Trivia

Pittsburgh Steelers Football

583) Bill Cowher was named head coach of the Pittsburgh Steelers in 1992.

   A) True
   B) False

584) How many seasons did Cowher spend as the Steelers head coach?

585) During his NFL playing career Cowher played for ___ NFL teams.

586) He was a player for which NFL teams?

587) Where did Cowher play his collegiate football?

588) In which round of the NFL Draft was Cowher drafted?

Answers:

583) A – True; Jan. 21
584) 15; He resigned on Jan. 5, 2007
585) Two
586) Philadelphia Eagles and Cleveland Browns
587) North Carolina State
588) None; Signed as a free agent

Progressive Trivia

Pittsburgh Steelers Football

589) How many times has Ben Roethlisberger passed for 300 or more yards in a game?

590) Does he hold the Steelers' record for the category?

591) Big Ben has more than twice as many 300-yard passing games as the No. 2 man on the list.

    A) True
    B) False

592) Where does Terry Bradshaw rank on the list?

593) Terry Bradshaw had ____ career 300-yard passing games.

594) Did Kordell Stewart ever pass for 300 or more yards in a game?

Answers:

589) 15
590) Yes
591) A – True; Tommy Maddox, 6
592) No. 4
593) Four
594) Yes, Three times

Progressive Trivia

Pittsburgh Steelers Football

595) How many times have the Steelers come back from a 21-point deficit to win a game?

596) What year did this first occur?

597) What was the final score of the contest?

598) Against which rival was the second occurrence?

599) The year was _____.

600) What was the final score of the game?

Answers:

595) Two
596) 1985
597) Steelers 30, Bills 24
598) Baltimore Ravens
599) 1997
600) Steelers 42, Ravens 34

Progressive Trivia

Pittsburgh Steelers Football

601) Which team is a party to the Steelers' team record for the most points combined?

    A) New England Patriots
    B) Arizona Cardinals
    C) Tennessee Titans
    D) San Diego Chargers

602) What year did the teams combine to set this record?

603) How many combined points did they score?

604) The game was played in _____.

605) Did the teams also combine for greater than 1,000 total yards?

606) Who left the field with a victory that day?

Answers:

601) D – San Diego Chargers
602) 1985; Dec. 8
603) 98
604) San Diego
605) No; 875 total yards combined
606) San Diego, 54-44

Progressive Trivia

Pittsburgh Steelers Football

607) Who holds the Steelers' record for the most career fumble recoveries?

   A) Jack Lambert
   B) Ernie Stautner
   C) Jack Ham
   D) Donnie Shell

608) How many career fumble recoveries did he have?

609) Did he score any touchdowns as a result of his fumble recoveries?

610) He began his career in Pittsburgh in 1950 and ended it in _____.

611) Who sits in the No. 2 spot on the Steelers' career list for the category?

612) How many career fumble recoveries did it take him to earn the No. 2 spot?

Answers:

607) B – Ernie Stautner
608) 23
609) No
610) 1963
611) Jack Ham
612) 21; 1971-82

Progressive Trivia

Pittsburgh Steelers Football

613) The Steelers' team record for the most net yards gained passing is _____.

614) Was this record set before or after the 1970 NFL-AFL merger?

615) Which of these teams gave up the passing yards?

   A) Chicago Cardinals
   B) San Francisco 49ers
   C) Philadelphia Eagles
   D) Chicago Bears

616) Who was the Steelers' quarterback that record-setting day?

617) How many passing attempts did he have in the game?

618) How many TD passes did he have that day?

Answers:

613) 472
614) Before; Dec. 13, 1958
615) A – Chicago Cardinals
616) Bobby Layne
617) 49
618) Two

Progressive Trivia

Pittsburgh Steelers Football

619) Have the Steelers played more than or fewer than five times on Thanksgiving Day?

620) Have the Steelers played the same team in each of those Thanksgiving Day appearances?

621) Which opponent have they faced twice on Thanksgiving Day?

622) When was the most recent season the Steelers made a Thanksgiving Day appearance?

623) Home many of the Steelers' Thanksgiving Day games have been played in Pittsburgh?

624) What is the Steelers' overall record on Thanksgiving Day?

Answers:

619) Fewer than; Three
620) No; Detroit Lions and Dallas Cowboys
621) Detroit Lions
622) 1998; Nov. 26
623) Zero
624) 0-3

Progressive Trivia

Pittsburgh Steelers Football

625) What university did Terry Bradshaw attend?

   A) Georgia Tech
   B) Virginia Tech
   C) Louisiana Tech
   D) Texas Tech

626) Ben Roethlisberger attended Miami University in Ohio.

   A) True
   B) False

627) Did Kordell Stewart go to college at Colorado State University?

628) Neil O'Donnell played quarterback for the _____.

629) Where did Bubby Brister play his college football?

630) Was Bobby Layne a Red Raider or Longhorn?

Answers:

625) C – Louisiana Tech
626) A – True
627) No; University of Colorado Boulder
628) Maryland Terrapins
629) Northeast Louisiana
630) Longhorn; University of Texas

Progressive Trivia

Pittsburgh Steelers Football

631) Who set the Steelers' record for the most touchdowns on interceptions in a game?

632) What season did he set the record?

633) Against which team did he set the record?

    A) Baltimore Ravens
    B) Kansas City Chiefs
    C) Tennessee Oilers
    D) Jacksonville Jaguars

634) How many touchdowns on interceptions did he have in the game?

635) Were both returns shorter than or longer than 50 yards?

636) How many yards was the longer of the two interception returns?

Answers:

631) Dewayne Washington
632) 1998; Nov. 22
633) D – Jacksonville Jaguars
634) Two
635) Longer than
636) 78; The other was 52 yards.

Progressive Trivia

Pittsburgh Steelers Football

637) Who did the Steelers play in Super Bowl XIV?

638) Where was the game contested?

639) The game's attendance exceeded 100,000.

   A) True
   B) False

640) Did the Steelers lead the entire game?

641) What was the score when the final seconds ticked off the clock?

642) Who was named Super Bowl XIV's Most Valuable Player?

Answers:

637) Los Angeles Rams
638) Rose Bowl Stadium, Pasadena, Calif.
639) A – True; 103,985
640) No
641) Steelers 31, Rams 19
642) Terry Bradshaw

Pittsburgh Steelers Football

643) How many Steelers have earned First Team All-Pro selections six times in their careers?

644) Jack Ham earned his sixth selection in which year?

645) Jack Lambert was named First Team All-Pro for the sixth time in _____.

646) Alan Faneca earned his sixth First Team All-Pro selection in 2008.

   A) True
   B) False

647) Did Dermontti Dawson receive his sixth First Team All-Pro selection in 1998?

648) How many times has Troy Polamalu been named First Team All-Pro?

Answers:

643) Four
644) 1979
645) 1983
646) B – False; 2007
647) Yes
648) Three; 2005, 2008 and 2010

Progressive Trivia

Pittsburgh Steelers Football

649) What is the Steelers' record for the most yards on kickoff returns in a career?

650) Which Steeler set this team record?

651) How many seasons did he spend in Pittsburgh?

652) _____ was his last season in the gold and black.

653) How many kickoff returns did he have in his career with the Steelers?

654) How many other NFL teams did he play with after leaving Pittsburgh?

    A) 0
    B) 2
    C) 3
    D) 4

Answers:

649) 4,894
650) Rod Woodson
651) 10
652) 1996
653) 220
654) C – 3; 49ers, Ravens and Raiders

Progressive Trivia

Pittsburgh Steelers Football

655) What is the record attendance for a game at Heinz Field?

656) Was this set at a regular-season or postseason game?

657) This record was set in _____.

658) Who was the Steelers' opponent that game?

659) Was the record crowd treated to a Steelers victory?

660) What was the contest's final score?

Answers:

655) 66,662
656) Postseason
657) 2011; 2010 season playoff game
658) New York Jets
659) Yes
660) Steelers 24, Jets 19

Progressive Trivia

Pittsburgh Steelers Football

661) Jerome Bettis owns the Steelers' career rushing record for the most rushing touchdowns.

   A) True
   B) False

662) How many rushing TDs did he score while in Pittsburgh?

663) What seasons did he don the black and gold?

664) Who is No. 2 on the career list for the most rushing TDs?

665) How many career rushing touchdowns did he score?

666) How many seasons did it take him to accumulate his rushing TDs?

Answers:

661) B – False; Franco Harris
662) 91
663) 1972-83
664) Jerome Bettis
665) 78
666) 10

Progressive Trivia

Pittsburgh Steelers Football

667) What is the name of the Steelers' costumed mascot?

668) He was introduced to Steeler Nation in _____.

669) How was his name chosen?

670) How many names were considered?

671) Who submitted the winning name?

672) The new mascot was introduced as part of the team's 75th anniversary festivities.

    A) True
    B) False

Answers:

667) Steely McBeam
668) 2007
669) A name-the-mascot contest
670) 70,000-plus
671) Diane Roles
672) A – True

Progressive Trivia

Pittsburgh Steelers Football

673) Where is the Steelers' annual summer training camp held?

674) In what city can it be found?

675) Steelers training camp was first held there in _____.

676) What is the name of the field at the camp?

677) What is the name of the traveling trailer that fans can visit during the training camp?

678) What long-time Steelers tradition takes place during dinners at the summer training camp?

Answers:

673) St. Vincent's College
674) Latrobe, Pa.
675) 1967
676) Chuck Noll Field
677) Traveling Great Hall
678) Rookie Singing; talent contest

Progressive Trivia

Pittsburgh Steelers Football

679) What year was the Steelers' record for the most yards on punt returns set?

    A) 1973
    B) 1984
    C) 1995
    D) 2006

680) Who set the record that season?

681) He had _____ punt return yards that year.

682) Who sits in the No. 2 spot on the Steelers' list for the category?

683) How many punt return yards did he amass to earn his No. 2 ranking?

684) What year did the No. 2 man earn his spot?

Answers:

679) B – 1984
680) Louis Lipps
681) 656
682) Lynn Swann
683) 577
684) 1974

Progressive Trivia

Pittsburgh Steelers Football

685) Gary Anderson holds the Steelers' career record for the most field goals made.

  A) True
  B) False

686) Does Gary Anderson have three times as many career field goals as Jeff Reed?

687) _____ sits in the No. 3 spot on the Steelers' career list for the most field goals.

688) How many field goals did he make?

689) Is Norm Johnson ranked in the top five on this list?

690) How many career field goals did Norm Johnson make?

Answers:

685) A – True; 309
686) No; He only has 50 percent more, 309:204
687) Roy Gerela
688) 146
689) Yes; Fourth
690) 105

Progressive Trivia

Pittsburgh Steelers Football

691) In 2001, _____ tied the Steelers' record for the longest pass play .

692) Who received the pass on the play?

693) How many yards did the play go?

694) How many other Steelers quarterback-receiver combinations have gone 90 yards on a pass play?

695) When did the second most recent 90-yard pass play take place?

696) Which pair represents the last of the three-way tie?

Answers:

691) Kordell Stewart
692) Bobby Shaw; Dec. 16, 2001, at Baltimore
693) 90
694) Two
695) 1990; Oct. 14, at Denver
696) T. Bradshaw and Mark Malone; Nov. 8, 1981 at Seattle

Progressive Trivia

Pittsburgh Steelers Football

697) The most completed passes by a Steelers QB in a game are _____.

698) Against which team was this record set?

699) Which Steelers quarterback owns the record?

700) What year did the game take place?

701) Who holds the No. 2 spot on this list?

   A) Neil O'Donnell
   B) Tommy Maddox
   C) Terry Bradshaw
   D) Joe Gilliam

702) How many passes did he complete in a single game to capture his No. 2 ranking?

Answers:

697) 38
698) Denver Broncos
699) Ben Roethlisberger
700) 2006; Nov. 5
701) A – Neil O'Donnell
702) 34; Nov. 5, 1995, at Chicago

Progressive Trivia

Pittsburgh Steelers Football

703) Where was Chuck Noll's place of birth?

704) Where did he attend college?

705) What year was he drafted?

706) Chuck Noll played quarterback for the Flyers.

    A) True
    B) False

707) What year did Chuck Noll coach his first game as the Steelers head coach?

708) Did he ever have another head coaching position in the NFL?

Answers:

703) Cleveland, Ohio
704) University of Dayton
705) 1953
706) B – False; Guard and Linebacker
707) 1969
708) No; He was an assistant and coordinator.

Progressive Trivia

Pittsburgh Steelers Football

709) Do Steelers players wear helmet numbers during the preseason?

710) All official captains of NFL teams wear "C" patches on their jerseys.

   A) True
   B) False

711) What does Troy Polamalu have embroidered near the neckline of the back of his jersey?

712) Which university approached the Steelers in 1979 to get permission to model their uniforms after the Steelers?

713) Steelers jerseys from which seasons are referred to as Batman jerseys?

714) For which Super Bowl did the Steelers choose to wear their white travel uniforms despite being the designated home team?

Answers:

709) No; Helmet numbers are used only after the final cut.
710) B – False; Steelers captains have never worn them.
711) A cross; It is usually hidden by his long hair.
712) Iowa, The Hawkeyes have worn them ever since.
713) 1966-67
714) Super Bowl XL

Progressive Trivia

Pittsburgh Steelers Football

715) Who played the most seasons as a Steeler?

716) _____ players have played 14 seasons in Pittsburgh.

717) Does Mike Webster also own the record for the most games played as a Steeler?

718) Who has played the second most games in black and gold?

719) What is Mike Webster's career record for the most consecutive games played in Pittsburgh?

720) Dermontti Dawson played the second most consecutive games for the Steelers.

   A) True
   B) False

Answers:

715) Mike Webster; 15
716) Six; Shell, Stallworth, L. Brown, Blount, Bradshaw and Stautner
717) Yes; 220
718) Hines Ward
719) 177; 1974-85
720) A – True; 170, 1988-99

Progressive Trivia

All information in this book is valid as of the end of the 2010 season.